LIGHTNING
BOLT
BOOKS™

Explore Neptune

Jackie Golusky

Lerner Publications • Minneapolis

PAGE PLUS +

Scan the QR code on page 21 to see Neptune in 3D!

Lerner Publications Company
An imprint of Lerner Publishing Group, Inc.
241 First Avenue North
Minneapolis, MN 55401 USA

For reading levels and more information, look up this title at www.lernerbooks.com.

Main body text set in Billy Infant regular.
Typeface provided by SparkType.

Library of Congress Cataloging-in-Publication Data

Names: Golusky, Jackie, 1996- author.
Title: Explore Neptune / Jackie Golusky.
Other titles: Lightning bolt books. Planet explorer.
Description: Minneapolis, MN : Lerner Publications, [2021] | Series: Lightning bolt books - Planet explorer | Includes bibliographical references and index. | Audience: Ages 6-9 | Audience: Grades 2-3 | Summary: "Did you know that Neptune is the windiest planet in the solar system? Discover more about Neptune in this exciting look at the farthest planet from the sun"— Provided by publisher.
Identifiers: LCCN 2020018200 (print) | LCCN 2020018201 (ebook) | ISBN 9781728404127 (library binding) | ISBN 9781728423647 (paperback) | ISBN 9781728418483 (ebook)
Subjects: LCSH: Neptune (Planet)—Juvenile literature.
Classification: LCC QB691 .G658 2021 (print) | LCC QB691 (ebook) | DDC 523.48—dc23

LC record available at https://lccn.loc.gov/2020018200
LC ebook record available at https://lccn.loc.gov/2020018201

Manufactured in the United States of America
1-48470-48984-6/29/2020

Table of Contents

All about Neptune

On Neptune, powerful winds blast. These winds can reach up to 1,200 miles (1,931 km) per hour. Neptune is the windiest planet in our solar system.

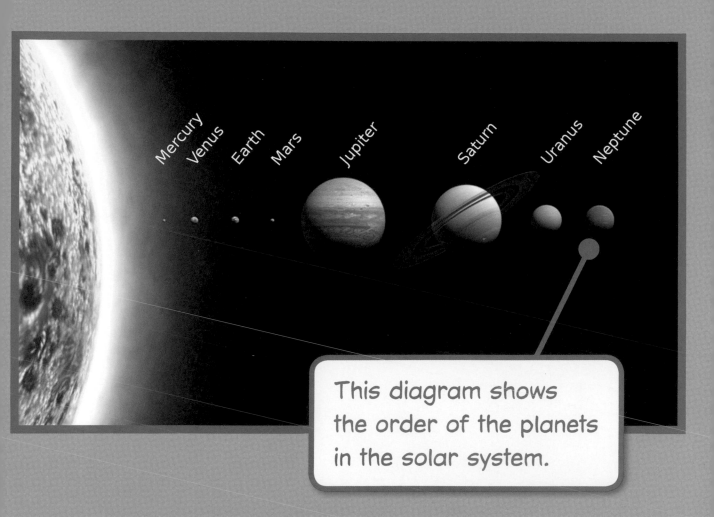

Mercury Venus Earth Mars Jupiter Saturn Uranus Neptune

This diagram shows the order of the planets in the solar system.

Neptune is the eighth and final planet in the solar system. It is about 2.8 billion miles (4.5 billion km) away from the sun. That means Neptune is thirty times farther from the sun than Earth is!

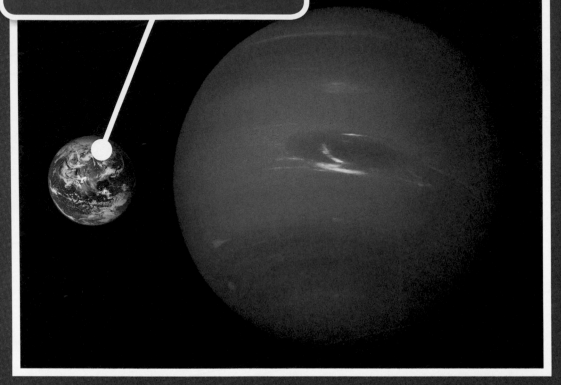

This diagram shows Earth (*left*) compared in size to Neptune.

Neptune is massive. It is 30,598 miles (49,244 km) across, while Earth is 7,918 miles (12,743 km) across. About four Earths could line up across Neptune.

Neptune has a frozen, icy core that is made of mostly water. Scientists call the planet an ice giant because of its extreme cold and huge size.

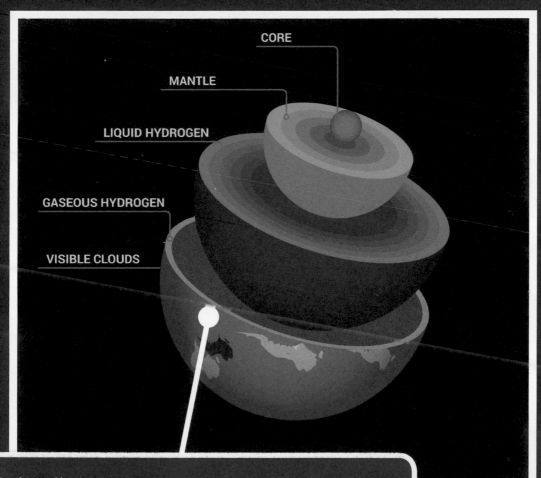

CORE

MANTLE

LIQUID HYDROGEN

GASEOUS HYDROGEN

VISIBLE CLOUDS

This diagram shows the layers of Neptune. Its outer gas layers are made of a material called hydrogen.

Neptune's Moons and Rings

Neptune has fourteen moons. Its largest moon is Triton. Triton is even bigger than the dwarf planet Pluto.

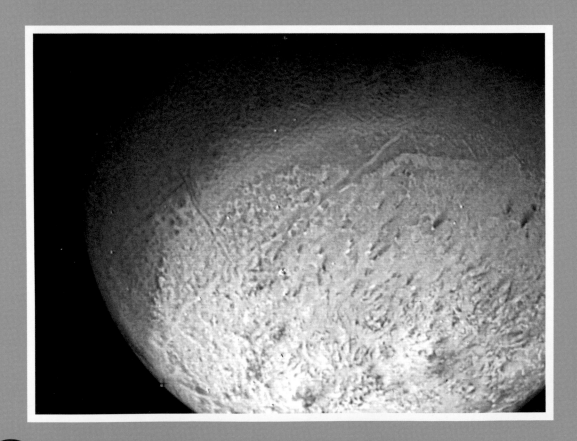

If you stood on Triton, Neptune would look huge in the sky.

Triton orbits Neptune the opposite way from Neptune's other moons. Scientists think Triton was an asteroid that wandered too close to Neptune. Neptune's powerful gravity pulled Triton into orbit.

Scientists think Neptune's rings formed when some of its moons crashed together and broke into pieces.

Neptune has five rings. Its rings are made of dust and small rocks. The rings are hard to see because they are very dark.

Neptune's rings are not like other rings in our solar system. Their rocks and dust clump together to form arcs. In 2005, astronomers discovered that one of Neptune's arcs is disappearing. They want to find out why.

Two of Neptune's rings shine in this photo taken by *Voyager 2*. The slightly brighter sections of the outer ring are called arcs.

Living on Neptune

If you were to visit Neptune, you would find a world that is very different from Earth. Neptune does not have a solid surface, so you cannot stand on it. Under its thick atmosphere is a slushy ocean.

Tall white clouds rise high above Neptune's atmosphere. They travel across the planet at high speeds.

Neptune has seasons. But the seasons are very different from Earth's. It takes Neptune 165 years to complete one orbit, and each of its seasons lasts for over 40 years!

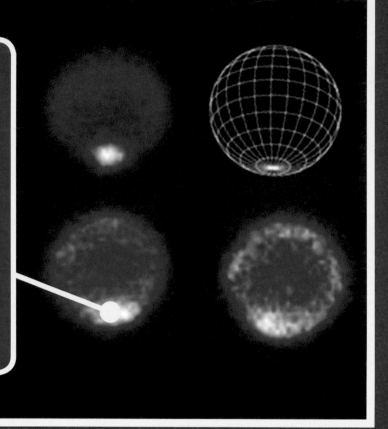

Scientists took images of Neptune's temperature and found that the planet's south pole (*white spot*) is warmer than the rest of it.

Neptune's average temperature is a frigid -353°F (-214°C), making it the coldest planet in the solar system. But Neptune also has a very thick atmosphere that traps heat deep down near its surface.

Some scientists think Neptune has an extremely hot ocean on its surface. They believe that the planet's thick atmosphere creates heavy pressure that keeps the water from boiling away.

Neptune has wild weather. Scientists think its rain is made of solid diamonds!

Checking Out Neptune

The first and only spacecraft to ever visit Neptune was *Voyager 2*. In 1989, the spacecraft flew by Neptune and studied its rings and moons.

The storms on Neptune are called dark spots.

Voyager 2 discovered huge storms on Neptune. Five years later, scientists tried to use the Hubble Space Telescope to learn more about these storms, but the storms were gone.

Since Neptune is so far away, it is hard to study it. NASA hopes to find out more about it. The James Webb Space Telescope will study objects in outer space, including Neptune.

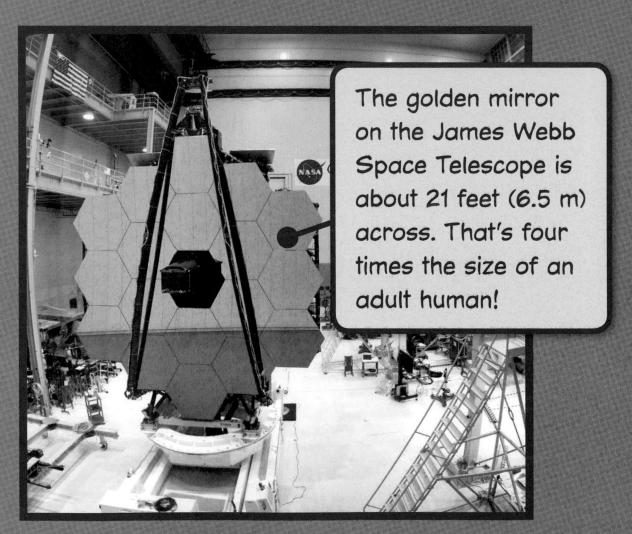

The golden mirror on the James Webb Space Telescope is about 21 feet (6.5 m) across. That's four times the size of an adult human!

The James Webb Space Telescope is so big that it has to be folded up for launch.

With the help of the James Webb Space Telescope, scientists will discover more about our most distant neighbor and its mysterious storms.

Planet Facts

- Neptune's winds are nine times stronger than Earth's.

- Neptune is named after the Greek god of the sea. Its moons are also named after gods and goddesses. Some of the names are Hippocamp, Nereid, Thalassa, and Proteus.

- Neptune gets its blue color from the methane in its atmosphere. Methane is a gas, like air.

Space Story

People disagree on who discovered Neptune. Galileo drew Neptune twice in 1613, and some say that he discovered it. Others say that Galileo did not discover it because it's unclear if he thought it was a star or planet. Astronomers are looking at Galileo's sketches to help settle the debate.

Scan the QR code to the right to see Neptune in 3D!

Glossary

arc: a section of a ring around Neptune made of clumps of dust and rock

asteroid: a large, rocky object that travels through the solar system

atmosphere: the air that surrounds a planet

orbit: to travel around an object in a circular or oval path

pressure: the action of pressing or pushing against something else

solar system: a star and the planets that move around it

spacecraft: a vehicle that travels in outer space

surface: the outer layer of land or water

Learn More

Ducksters: Astronomy
https://www.ducksters.com/science/solarsystem.php

Golusky, Jackie. *Explore Uranus.* Minneapolis: Lerner Publications, 2021.

Jones, Emma. *Exploring Neptune.* New York: KidHaven, 2018.

Kiddle: Neptune's Moons
https://kids.kiddle.co/List_of_Neptune%27s_moons

Murray, Julie. *Neptune.* Minneapolis: Abdo Zoom, 2019.

NASA: All about Neptune
https://spaceplace.nasa.gov/all-about-neptune/en/

Index

Photo Acknowledgments

Image credits: NASA/ARC, p. 4; WP/Wikimedia Commons (CC BY-SA 3.0), p. 5; Orange-kun/ Wikimedia, p. 6; Mevan/Shutterstock.com, p. 7; NASA/JPL, pp. 8, 11, 13, 14, 16, 17; NASA/ JPL/USGS, p. 9; Dotted Yeti/Shutterstock.com, p. 10; NASA/JPL-Caltech, p. 12; Bjoern Wylezich/Shutterstock.com, p. 15; NASA/GSFC, pp. 18, 19.

Cover: Ian McKinnell/Getty Images.